Jerusalem Journey

Jerusalem Journey

Jared Pinkney

XULON PRESS

Xulon Press
2301 Lucien Way #415
Maitland, FL 32751
407.339.4217
www.xulonpress.com

© 2022 by Jared Pinkney

All rights reserved solely by the author. The author guarantees all contents are original and do not infringe upon the legal rights of any other person or work. No part of this book may be reproduced in any form without the permission of the author.

Due to the changing nature of the Internet, if there are any web addresses, links, or URLs included in this manuscript, these may have been altered and may no longer be accessible. The views and opinions shared in this book belong solely to the author and do not necessarily reflect those of the publisher. The publisher therefore disclaims responsibility for the views or opinions expressed within the work.

Paperback ISBN-13: 978-1-66285-497-2
Hard Cover ISBN-13: 978-1662859-28-1
Ebook ISBN-13: 978-166285-498-9

In Memory of Nathaniel Jordan Barnes

Back in the days of Nehemiah, there lived a man in Persia by the name of Samuel. This was a time in Samuel's life that was very happy and joyful because he was comfortable living where he was, with just himself and his wife. Things seemed simple and easy, and if they could remain how they were, then he would have no problem with that at all.

Samuel was a man of deep thought and strong ambition. He was a soft-spoken dreamer who constantly questioned his own thoughts and actions. Samuel often found that he would talk to himself aloud without even realizing it. It was as if his mind had a mind of its own, and he couldn't control his thoughts or his feelings.

Samuel's wife's name was Rachel. She was truly the apple of his eye. Samuel was the sheep, and Rachel was the lion. She was outspoken and fierce in her demeanor. Rachel was sweet, yet strong. She was loud, yet humble. Samuel and Rachel were very much in love with each other. But outside of that was an even greater love. They loved God more than they loved each other. They knew if they loved God, then everything else would fall into place.

One night, God spoke to Samuel in a dream. God told Samuel to take his wife and travel to Jerusalem to help build a wall around the city that was being built during this time period. Samuel was promised a better life than what he had now, although the journey there might be treacherous. When Samuel woke the next morning, he felt troubled by the dream because he was so comfortable in his current disposition in life.

Samuel and Rachel lived on a small farm. Samuel was doing his daily duties around the farm, all while pondering what to do about his dream. By the end of the day, he decided to tell his wife the message he had received from the Lord. By this time, he had already made up his mind that he would obey. Rachel rejected the idea because of the comfort of her current lifestyle. Samuel explained, "If you don't trust me on this, you don't trust God on this matter. For it was God who instructed me on this journey, and I'll obey Him regardless of if you accompany me or not." With that said, Rachel agreed to go on the journey as well. They started making preparations.

The next day, Samuel and Rachel got up early and put as many supplies inside their wagon as they could fit. They chose the strongest horse they had and made sure he had plenty to eat before the departure. Nehemiah was a man granted permission by God to lead people out of the territory of Persia. Nehemiah led the Jews from Persia to Jerusalem to build a wall around the city. Nehemiah had already left weeks ago with a wave of people he was taking to Jerusalem. It would have been ideal for the couple to have gone with Nehemiah and his wave of people, but this journey would have to be accomplished with just the two of them. Samuel made sure to tell his neighbors that they could have the farm because he and Rachel wouldn't be coming back. By the end of the day, all of their knots had been tied. All that was left was to get a good night's rest and start their journey early the next morning. Samuel dreamed he was lost in a strange land with no direction.

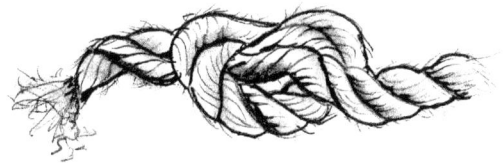

Lost In Questions

"I fly into the abyss of the unknown.
Unwavering potential and unmovable motivation drive me forward at an expeditious rate.
Accelerating while blind can be dangerous.
But I like the rush.
Mysterious signals capture my attention and direct me to something different.
I divert my attention to several locations to seek the possibilities of what's next.
Being open to last-minute changes is a must.
I have a quick pivot.
Anxiousness loves to cling to my chest while I turn the knobs to brand new doors just to see if they're locked.
I question my questions.

Jerusalem Journey

Indecisively making decisions puts me at a standstill.
Hesitation might be the death of me.
I'm unsure."

The next morning was subtle and quiet. The horse and wagon were full and ready to go, so Samuel and Rachel got in the wagon and were on their way. The horse pulled the wagon at a steady pace. Rachel questioned Samuel about this journey. She wanted specifics as to where exactly they would live, how long it would take to get there, and what Jerusalem would be like. Samuel told her that this was a walk of faith, and he didn't have the answers to those questions. Samuel wondered these things as well, but he kept that to himself.

God told Samuel to take a different route to Jerusalem than that of Nehemiah. He did as was instructed. This route was unfamiliar to most, and Samuel didn't know what was ahead, but there seemed to be a storm in the distance. As the young couple traveled toward the storm, Samuel had feelings of uncertainty. He hoped they could find a safe place to shelter themselves from the storm. The clouds were dark, and the air was moist. Samuel pondered about what was to come.

Dread

"What's this?
This ominous feeling of impending danger and persecution heavily breathes on the back of my neck.
A creepy sensation of carnage and treachery seems to lightly tickle my skin.
I'm nervous.
My boldness seems to have taken off without me.
Fire has been ignited in the lower pit of my stomach as a warning signal to myself and any intruder along the way. I worry for the things unseen and unheard for I fear undeserved punishment and torture."

Samuel and Rachel came across a cave that they thought looked like a suitable place for them to stay the night. They unloaded some of their things and built a fire. They had plenty of food and water. They ate, drank, and talked around the fire, discussing the possibilities of why God would have had them to move so suddenly. Samuel explained that having faith in God sometimes involved not knowing or fully understanding His plans. It began to rain throughout the night, and the couple slept very peacefully.

The next day, they got an early start on the road. They passed several people going the opposite way. In the afternoon, they stopped to talk to an old merchant standing on the side of the road. Samuel carried their money in his little bag that he kept in his pocket. He paid the merchant for some bread and water. The merchant said, "You'll be needing this for the journey ahead. The land that lies before you starts to become more open and desolate." The couple took heed of the man's words and went on their way. Samuel began to ponder on if he had really heard from God or not. He wondered if he'd made the right decision.

Indecisive

"I continue to vacillate between my present state and past decisions.
I don't have clarity of mind, and my thoughts are riddles that don't entertain me.
My emotions stay hidden to show strength and certainty.
At times, I think I've fooled even myself.
A coin that has two heads and continues to spin can be very perplexing. Confusion leads to illusion.
This dizzy heart of mine grows tired and abruptly dazed by unusual circumstances."

Foreign

"I've never been a part of this.
I'm incongruous to the people and their culture.
Unfamiliar land rejects me and puts my body in a state of stress and discomfort.
The things I cherish I cannot share.
Traditions and routines don't settle comfortably with me.
They degrade my ways of life, and they've never heard of my homeland.
They don't know where I'm coming from.
The love I carry for the things I hold dear continues to stay close to me.
I don't belong here."

Samuel and Rachel began to travel through very mountainous terrain. It was beautiful. The sun was shining, and the birds were singing. The air was refreshing, and it wasn't too hot. Rachel wanted to stop and have a picnic in a small crevice in the mountain where they had a great view. They stopped and ate merrily as they talked about their friends back home. They very much missed their old life, but they trusted God with their new one.

The couple heard a rustle in the bush behind them. The couple turned around to find a man with battered clothes and a long, dark beard carrying a small bag and a stick. He stood there with a solemn expression and a look of despair. He introduced himself as John and explained that he was almost home, but he was out of food and water, and he asked if he could he have some for the road. Samuel and Rachel didn't mind sharing. In fact, they invited him to sit down and eat with them. They had plenty of food to spare, so it wasn't a big sacrifice. Rachel explained to John how God had instructed her husband to leave and go to Jerusalem.

John asked, "If there really is a God, then why would He allow such evil things to take place here on earth?"

Rachel replied, "Well it depends on what you mean by 'evil.' In order to call something or someone evil, you would also have to have the concept of good. You're implying that things should be a certain way. How do you know which way things should be unless you have an objective standpoint of morality? If you're making moral decisions based off your own feelings, then that doesn't cut it. The only way to truly justify our morals is through God, the Creator of all living things. If He created us, then He also created our morals. If He didn't create us, then this 'evil' that you speak of is merely your opinion of something that should or shouldn't be a certain way."

John didn't have a response. He seemed to be in deep thought about Rachel's words. Samuel smiled as he never ceased to be amazed at his wife's insight, and he felt so glad that he'd married her. John prepared to continue on his way, but the couple got him some food and water for him to take on his journey back home. He thanked them and continued his own journey. Samuel and Rachel gathered their things and continued their journey as well.

The journey down the mountain was gracious and relaxing. Rachel and Samuel told stories and reminisced about when they were kids. Their journey took them through some flat land in an area populated with many trees. With the mountains now behind them, they journeyed through what seemed to be a forest. Rachel wanted to stop to eat a snack near a small creek that she spotted. Samuel thought it to be a good idea, so they sat by the creek and ate. They rejoiced and worshipped God for His goodness. Rachel pondered and spoke on how God's goodness is perfect even if they didn't fully understand it. She had been very hesitant and skeptical when her husband had first told her about going on this journey, and now she was all in.

Samuel and Rachel finished their snack and continued their journey through the woods. As they rode in the wagon, Samuel realized it was getting dark. He figured it would be best if they got off the road and pulled over in the grass to get some sleep. Samuel saw a nice spot to sleep, and Rachel suggested they get an early start in the morning. That night, Samuel had a terrible dream of persecution. He was in a small village, and he'd been beaten and pulled out in the street to be stoned. He was left with just his last few thoughts.

Reminisce

"The humiliation seeps through my pores for everyone to see and taste.
My resolve has had an incomplete resolution to a journey that was once expedited by a strong pursuit of endless purpose and persuasion.
My passion runs dry and loses its stamina due to the reckless actions of those who continue to plot against me.
These last moments I'll hold dear for the things and people I truly cherish.
They're embedded in my memory.
My blood awaits to take impact on the ground beneath me and share my secrets with the feet of those who walk upon this location.
Indignation rises as I fall.
I'll wither away, but the truth will remain firm, regardless of the human intervention that wishes to morph reality.
This is the last of me, and all I'll be is a memory."

Samuel and Rachel continued to travel through the forest. There was an old woman along the side of the road picking flowers. When the couple rode up beside her, the old lady asked where they were going. Rachel told the lady how God had instructed them to move to Jerusalem to help build the wall. The old lady said, "God's not real, and there's no way to prove that He exists. What a silly notion you both have."

Rachel replied to the lady by asking her why she was picking flowers. The old lady said, "I feel it's my calling to pick these beautiful flowers and sell them to the people of my town. Some of the best flowers grow in this forest, and I think it's what I was called to do so that I can contribute to bringing people happiness."

Rachel put on a bold smile and said, "Ma'am, if there's no God, then there is no purpose for your life at all. As a matter of fact, there's no purpose for anyone's life. You mentioned bringing people happiness. Well, what makes you think this is something you should be doing? Did someone tell you to do this? Why would bringing people happiness be a good thing, and how do you know that it's good? Everything that's created has a purpose. God created us to be creatures of purpose. Without Him, then everything is really just a series of things that occur, some being more desirable than others. You're not called to pick these flowers; you're just simply doing it."

After Rachel finished her last sentence, she gave Samuel a nudge to continue on their journey. The wagon started to pull away from the old lady. Samuel wasn't too surprised at how straightforward his wife had been with the woman. Rachel had always been that way, and Samuel loved that about her. As Samuel looked back, he saw the old lady drop her flowers and stare at the ground.

Samuel and Rachel made it through the forest and continued to make progress on their journey. They rode into a small town that seemed very desolate and impoverished. While Samuel and Rachel rode in the middle of town, they still didn't see anyone in sight. The sound of a door slamming came from the building to their right. There were three men dressed in ragged clothes walking out to interact with them on the dusty road.

Samuel stopped the horse and asked them why the town was so abandoned. The men walked up to the wagon and told them to hand over all of their valuables. Rachel replied, "How unbecoming of a man to try and steal from hard-working people just because you're too lazy to get out and go make something of yourself."

Normally, Samuel didn't mind his wife being so straightforward, but in this case, it caused Samuel a surge a panic because he didn't think they were dealing with patient, civilized men.

The first man grabbed Rachel from the wagon and threw her down in a sudden rage. Samuel quickly jumped out of the wagon to defend his wife. The first man was about to kick Rachel while she was on the ground, but Samuel punched him in the back of the head from behind. The second man came up behind Samuel and threw him to the ground. The third man rushed over to start kicking Samuel while he was curled up in the dirt.

Rachel got up and leaped for the man kicking Samuel, but before she could get to him, the first man struck her on the side of the face, knocking her to the ground once more. Samuel was on his feet again. He tried to get to Rachel but was quickly knocked down again after being hit across the head. Samuel and Rachel continued to get beaten while on the ground. It felt like the beating was taking a lifetime. The last thing the couple saw as they lay defenselessly on the ground was their wagon rolling away.

Samuel and Rachel were unconscious for hours. The sun started to set as he began to wake up. His vision was blurry, and his breathing was light. Samuel stared at the sky for a number of minutes due to his lack of strength. He was able to turn to his left where he saw Rachel lying about six feet away from him. She was all battered and bruised. Samuel was able to slowly inch his way over to her and look upon her face. His thoughts began to race.

Hollow

"One last phrase left her mouth as she gently faded away.
I call out to her as I lay face down, paralyzed in pain.
There will be no more quality time.
There will be no more conversations.
This happened in an instant, and I'm still perplexed as to why this has happened to me.
She lays cold and motionless
I nudge her with the last of my strength to see if she'll stir.
But that time has passed.
No more laughing.
No more crying.
No more sarcastic jokes.
The woman she once was no longer exists.
She's heard my voice for the last time.
She's hollow."

Unspoken

"A lump in my throat captures my voice.
I'm left with no thoughts or sounds on a motionless road.
The results of my productivity result in absolute zero.
My responsibilities have been defused out of my own accord.
These unspoken words never get to tell their own story.
Blank pages with no ink may be a story within itself.
Untold tales will never get the recognition they deserve.
Untouchable traces of untapped potential and mesmerizing design.
Thoughts in their purest forms fill the air and resonate within a timely manner.
Silence might be my greatest weapon."

Samuel wept over his wife's dead body in desperate agony. He couldn't accept the fact that he had allowed the love of his life to just be taken from him. Samuel couldn't comprehend that God would allow such a hateful act to be inflicted on people who were so innocent. Samuel felt like his whole body would break, not from the bumps and bruises, but from heartache. As of right now, all he knew was that Rachel was dead, and he wanted to die right beside her. Samuel faded away as he drifted to sleep on Rachel's body.

The next morning, Samuel woke up and had some strength to get on his feet. He looked around and found that the thieves had thrown one of his belongings on the ground. It was his bag. Inside of the bag was an empty bottle and a small notebook. He strapped the bag on his back and kissed his wife on the forehead as he solemnly said his last goodbye. Rachel had always told him that if she ever died before he did, she didn't want a proper funeral or burial because she knew that her earthly body would just be an empty shell. She knew where her spirit would be. The plan for the journey was still the same. Samuel would continue the journey alone. His thoughts began to take flight.

The Journey Continues

"I'm venturing on without you now.
I haven't fully finalized how to accomplish that task.
The new layout has several divisions that are still up for debate.
My to-do list has multiplied as well as my ambitions.
Nothing is really the same anymore.
This bitter taste in my mouth only sweetens when it falls down my throat.
My bag seems heavier than it used to be.
I have the necessary tools to accompany me whenever needed.
Maybe I won't get so lonely."

The Journey Continues II

"On and on the journey goes.
With no estimated time of arrival and a blurry vantage point.
My breathing is heavy, and I've come to a complete halt.
I just need some time to rest.
These prayers of mine seem to have no effect.
My screams of pain seem to be unheard.
Waves of thoughts capture my attention for hours.
My mind has rewarded me and kept me occupied in a different realm to help the time pass by a little faster.
Low is the valley and steep are the hills that hold my footprints behind me.
I don't know how much farther I'll go from here."

Without Direction

"I walk as aimlessly as any broken compass with
tired legs.
I've never been good at directions.
Wandering for this long almost makes things
seem normal.
It seems I have no clue as to where my life will take me.
Only questions.
Fear of the unknown always seeps through the surface
of my mind.
Yet, there's always a hint of excitement.
I continue writing pages in my mental book about this
long and cumbersome adventure.
Pain seems to be the ongoing theme."

Samuel continued to walk as long as his feet could carry him. He traveled down a long, winding road. His strength was depleted, and his motivation was running low. In the distance, he could see a small town. Samuel hoped he could find refuge there so that he could recover. He knew mustering up enough energy would be the hard part. It would take him the rest of the day to get to the small town.

When Samuel arrived in the town, he could barely stand. He didn't have much but the clothes on his back. There were not many people out on the streets, but the people who were outside were scattered abroad. They either gave him looks of concern or completely ignored him. Samuel veered off the road so he could walk near some of the homes in the town. He came across a big house with a horse stable. He saw several horses, and beside one of them was a middle-aged man with dark hair and round brown eyes. Samuel was just about to ask the man if he could spare any water. All of a sudden, everything started to go dark all around him. His head began to feel light, and his body began to feel weightless.

Samuel woke up in a small bedroom. He got out of bed and walked down the hallway and into the living room. The man from the stable greeted him with a kind smile and said, "Hello, my name is Jeremiah. I took the liberty of tending to your wounds. You can stay as long as you need to. I have food, water, and some extra clothes." Samuel introduced himself and began to weep. He told Jeremiah the story of him and his wife from the time they'd left Persia. The two men talked for about an hour. Jeremiah was able to empathize because his own wife had died several years ago of a disease. He explained how he had had to struggle with not being consumed by hatred. Jeremiah said, "Feel free to go get cleaned up. I have everything set up in the room across from where you were sleeping. When you finish, I'll have something prepared for you to eat."

Samuel came to the kitchen when he was finished bathing. Jeremiah set the table, and the food was hot and ready to eat. The two men sat and blessed the meal, and they ate pork, rice, and green beans. They talked for hours about their lives and how God had led them. Samuel spoke of the resentment of not being strong enough to save his wife. He spoke of the inner turmoil he felt about the indignation that had been allowed on his life by God. He expressed the sadness and hateful anger that had steered him in an unknown direction.

Jeremiah listened intently and said, "I understand your pain, but please don't let this hatred overtake you. It will eat away at your life and take you places you never wanted to go. Sometimes we don't know or understand why these things happen, but God knows the beginning to the end. I'll let you stay here for as long as you need. We brothers in Christ have to look out for one another, and even if we weren't brothers in Christ, we should still be looking out for one another." Samuel thanked him for his hospitality and assured him that he'd be on his way in one or two more days.

Two days later, Samuel was ready to continue his journey. Jeremiah gave Samuel food and water to put in his travel bag. Jeremiah also gave him a dagger to strap to his waist for protection. The last gift that was given to him was a horse. Samuel's heart began to swell as he knew these gifts were great sacrifices for Jeremiah, but Samuel was very grateful. Before he left, there was one last thing he wanted to get off his chest and share with Jeremiah.

Everything I Never Wanted

"This is the true depiction of the opposite attraction.
What I loathe finds its way into my bosom. And the
things I love seem to consistently evade me.
People I never wanted to meet seem to stay in
my company.
Places I've never wanted to go always seem to be my
first destination.
Unwanted gifts and consecutive days of abandonment.
Quizzical problems and unanswered questions.
Life never felt so confusing.
To catch a break is just wishful thinking.
I keep constantly sinking.
I can't seem to catch my breath."

Everything I Never Wanted II

"Finding what I seek doesn't seem possible in an illusion.
A false world of pixie dust and made-up realities.
And it's all made of plastic.
Jaded beyond belief with no drive or purpose.
Asking for help doesn't seem to help; but I guess I'm easy to ignore.
Things that used to please me no longer have the same appeal.
I'm becoming embedded into a foreign culture that shouldn't be familiar to me.
I've started to grow comfortable to the mundane life of an empty hunt.
I'm lost in the mix.
I've adjusted to a lifestyle that has always repulsed me because of its attributes.
But now I'm the most prominent part of a broken system."

Samuel gave Jeremiah a hug goodbye and went on his way. He rode off on his new horse and began to go through the town. There were more people out on the street today buying things from the market, teaching, and being merry with one another. Stumbling out of a small building near the end of the block were three men dressed in casual wear. Samuel's heart stopped as he immediately identified them to be the three men who had killed his wife. Rage surged through him as he contemplated his next move.

The three men were slightly drunk, and they seemed to be heading off the road and deeper into the town. Samuel decided to tie his horse to a nearby post and follow the men. He followed them for about ten minutes while being sure to stay hidden. The men went inside of a house and closed the door. After the men were inside for several minutes, Samuel chose to make a move. He was so furious that he could hardly think straight. Samuel kicked in the door and pulled his dagger from his side. He slayed all three men in a blind fury. Now, with new blood on his hands, he knew he had to leave town as quickly as possible. There wasn't much time to think, so he found his horse and rode out of town. Samuel pondered impure thoughts to himself as he traveled in silence.

Point of No Return

"Giving myself away to an unknown rage and a relentless darkness.
A new monster is born.
No more love.
No more crying.
No more resistance.
A new pathway has been paved under the circumstances of high pressure and low assistance.
I've given in.
I welcome these foreign feelings and deeply embedded instincts.
Fighting seems inevitable. I'll just redirect the combat.
I'll embrace this new armor and wear it like the latest fashion.
I don't care if it's over.
I've already turned."

Point Of No Return II

"I've let it consume me.
It's touched my conscience and reconstructed my entire frame.
This new shape that I've been molded into has assembled a new me.
Bloodthirst and mercilessness seem to be the necessity.
Fear my ambition and cower in helplessness as I proudly walk upon useless vessels.
Move aside and be amazed as I carry the world's burdens on my shoulders.
How many wrongs will I have to commit to make this right?"

Samuel continued to travel to Jerusalem at a steady pace. He traveled in silence throughout the day and drowned sorrow. He thought back on what he could have done differently to avoid the tragedy that became of his wife. He lingered on what his life would look like when he arrived in Jerusalem. Samuel began to question God and His authority. The confusion behind the ways of God just seemed to baffle him. Samuel made up in his mind that he would slaughter anyone else who got in his way from here on out.

Understanding

"Sadness is no stranger to me.
Loneliness keeps me company.
I spend time with no one else.
Acts of helplessness wave at me in the form of a withering rose as it bows its head in a sardonic fashion.
This emptiness needs to be quenched in the form of rejuvenation to hold me over until the last storm.
Seclusion surrounds me as I solemnly spectate the world from a hidden vantage point.
Productivity became nothing more than a redundant chore and an ill use of time.
I fell in love with idle hands.
An unreachable bond that sat close to me only by shadows of other bonds.
Pain begat more pain.
How many more wrongs will have to be done for me to make this right?
I just long for understanding."

Let It Be

―᧚᧙―

"If this is the end, then just let it be the end.
I've exhausted all other options, and I no longer
feel a thing.
My gifts have become stale and outdated.
The efforts to build my empire have become useless
and in vain.
The control has vacated my possession and left me ruler
of no one.
I can't get better, and I don't want to pick up the pieces.
If it's a disaster, then just let it be a disaster.
I'm beyond the reach of everyone who might wish to
assist me.1
I don't think I care.
No longer caring for my belongings; for they were
only things.
Let them burn.
I've lost compassion for the feelings of others.
Let them burn."

The sun was starting to go down, and Samuel was exhausted from the full day of travel. He found a big tree with large branches, and he tied his horse to the tree and settled down for the evening. He took the bread and some dried meat from his bag and started eating. Samuel had several bottles of fresh water, but he knew he had to use them sparingly. Surviving without food for a while is more probable than surviving without water.

The next morning, as Samuel traveled along the dirt road, he crossed paths with a merchant. The man was short with dark skin, sunken eyes, and a big hat, and he was selling food and water. Samuel hopped off of his horse and knocked the man unconscious. He took everything he could fit in his travel bag and rode away. Samuel could no longer cope with doing things the right way because he felt he had been wronged. He started to doubt God and question why someone who is all good and all-knowing would allow for this to happen to him, simply out of being obedient.

Samuel got on his horse and continued to ride down the trail while feeling the pain and regret of not being able to rescue his wife. The constant turmoil left him nauseous and lightheaded. As he continued to travel down the road, Samuel saw a small river. He decided to stop and relax in the river for a while to refresh himself.

Samuel laid in the river for what felt like hours. He contemplated while soaking in the water and taking in the sun. He got out of the water and began to dry off. While Samuel continued to dry off, a middle-aged man approached him from the other side of the river. "You mind if I sit with you for a while? I could use some good company," said the stranger. Samuel agreed to keep the man company. "Sometimes I come out here to pray and be alone with the Lord. This is a relaxing and comforting place for me." The man spoke with much passion and conviction, and that was touching to Samuel.

"What's your name?" Samuel asked.

"That doesn't matter. I just felt led to tell you that God loves you. I see the hate and pain in your eyes. You look like a man who has experienced true pain and loneliness. I just wanted to encourage you to keep pushing and don't give up." The stranger was caring and passionate when he spoke.

"Look, I've given God everything, and He did nothing but take from me in return. Being obedient to God isn't something that has truly worked out for me in the end. This isn't the way I pictured my life," Samuel replied.

The stranger took a few moments of silence to respond; then he spoke and said, "You're assuming that this is the end, and your journey hasn't even ended yet. Make sure that your script is only a rough draft."

"What do you mean?" Samuel inquired.

"Everyone has an unwritten script for their lives. This script is a blueprint of how they prefer things to be, whether it be regarding things, people, situations, or even yourself. Things are uncomfortable for us whenever something doesn't go according to our inner scripts. We try place people in roles in our scripts that they never signed up for to begin with. We try to control situations according to the layout of our scripts, and if it doesn't go according to plan, then it makes us uncomfortable or disappointed. Sometimes you need to let go and let God write the script. After all, it's really His play from the beginning."

Samuel was moved by the words of the man. He got up to get some water from his backpack that he'd left near his horse. Samuel was about to offer the man some water, but when he looked up, the stranger was gone. The horse began to stir and snap Samuel out of his trance. Before Samuel began to get on the trail again, he made sure his horse was well fed and had plenty of water. Then he was on his way again while pondering his current lifestyle.

Halt

─⊙⊃⊂⊙─

"I've stopped moving.
It's difficult for me to be stuck here for this long.
Tortured by the past and haunted by the future.
I find the things I once searched for unattainable on every path.
My decisions have become slow and indecisive.
I've stopped moving.
Delusions don't make things any easier for me.
It's hard to tell what's real.
Unorganized in all of my methods.
Sporadic adventures and unorthodox behavior are all I see around me.
Compassion has left me.
I've stopped moving.
A silent panic washes over me as I begin to accept reality.
People were once so beautiful.
Things seemed to have depth and meaning.
And now, all seems lost.
I've stopped moving."

It was starting to get dark, and Samuel found a nice spot on the side of the road. He got off of his horse and began to cry. He cried for the loss of his wife. He cried for the loss of the three men he had killed in a blind rage. He cried for the terrible thoughts that had poisoned his mind throughout the time of rebellion that ruled his heart. Rachel wouldn't have wanted him to go down a dark path of revenge and disobedience. Samuel asked God to fill in the loneliness, anger, and despair that was rooted in his heart. He cried himself to sleep.

The next morning, Samuel woke up with a new perspective. He had slept better that night than he had in a long time. God had touched him in a way that made him feel like everything would be alright. He continued down the road at a steady pace for the next several hours. The smell of moisture was in the air, and then the wind started to pick up. There was a nearby trail that forked off from the main road. Samuel could hear the crashing of waves in the distance, so he decided to veer off and take the trail for a short venture.

After about thirty minutes, Samuel stopped his horse and stared in awe. He'd found a beautiful beach. He tied his horse to a nearby tree and walked on the beach, kicking off his shoes and letting his toes frolic in the sand. It was such a delight to walk on the beach and taste the moisture in the air. Samuel ran to the ocean and kicked and screamed with joy. He decided to swim and enjoy the cool water while he had the opportunity. After he was finished swimming, Samuel got out of the water and just admired the beach. His heart began to overflow as he grasped a better comprehension of God's creativity. "If there's a work of art, then there must be an artist," he said.

Samuel looked over to the left of where he'd tied his horse, and he saw some berry bushes that must have slipped his sight when he'd first arrived. He was probably so excited when he first got on the beach that he just didn't see them.

Samuel ran over to pick the berries from the bush. He ate until he was full, and he grabbed his bag and started to pack it with berries. He picked all of the berries off of the bushes. They would probably last him for about two or three meals. Samuel tied his bag to his horse and walked over to a nice warm spot in the sand. His fingers tickled the sand as he pondered the omniscient power of God. He whispered, "God knows exactly how many grains of sand lay on this beach."

Samuel closed his eyes and listened to the waves crash upon the shore. He began to think of the depth of the ocean in comparison to God's love. Samuel whispered, "The ocean is deep, and the water swallows all who enter. As deep as this ocean is, it doesn't compare to the love of God by any means. The ocean's depth will end. God's love does not." As the warm sand continued to cradle Samuel's body, he drifted off into a deep sleep.

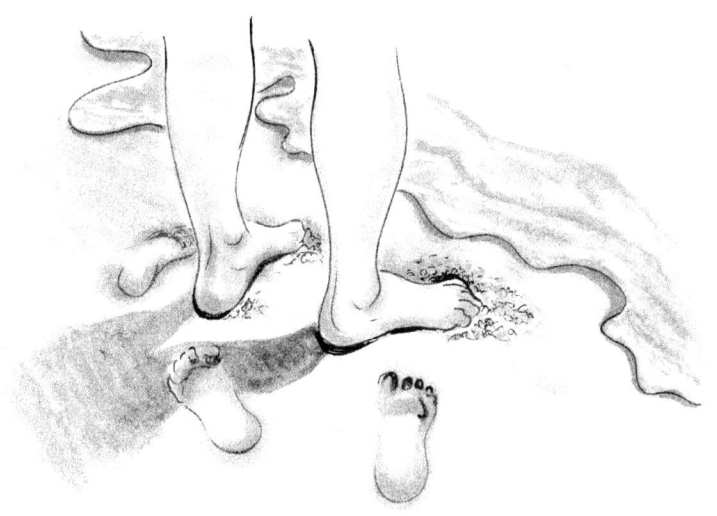

At Peace

―⸺෴⸺―

"I'm satisfied with the modified version of my current persona.
I've slept with solidified comprehension of true sorrow and expedient momentum.
Sweet sounds of nature continue to nurture me on this short sabbatical.
Laying lazily never felt so good.
The monstrosity of my destruction never seemed so far away."

Promised Land

"Happy moments and new beginnings pave a way for an overwhelming sense of joy and reassurance.
Lovely pleasures and unattained visions grace my presence with spotless beauty.
Please let this last.
Extensions of myself remain captured with the lovely individuals who I cherish most.
Lightly laying softly in a pile of saving grace and heightened positive ambition.
The best is yet to come."

Samuel woke up from a long nap. He stood up and saw that there seemed to be extra footprints in the sand that tracked back to where he'd left his horse. Samuel's mind started to race, and his pulse quickened. He ran back to where he'd tied his horse, only to find that the horse wasn't there. His bag was also gone. Someone had stolen his horse and his bag of belongings. The only thing they'd left behind was his little black notebook. Samuel walked back to the main road in utter confusion and defeat. Just when he thought things were getting better, they got worse all over again. He didn't know why God would allow him to feel such love and comfort in one moment and then in that same moment, allow for such an evil to bestow itself on him.

So he continued to walk as the sun was starting to set. He was angry that his obedience seemed to always be met with punishment. Samuel missed his wife, and he longed to see her again. The missing hole in his heart begged to be filled. The loss of his closest companion caused him an unfamiliar grief. Samuel walked off the road as the sun started to go down. He found a big bush that he hoped would keep him warm. He had nothing but himself and his old notebook, so he jumped in the bush and slightly hoped that maybe someone would come find him and put him out of his misery. His thoughts ran away on their own before he fell asleep.

Regretful Sorrow

"I truly miss her.
My heart sings a different tune, and it's completely off base.
I've lost sense of my senses.
I hope this distortion continues so none of this is real.
Living with a new reality doesn't seem manageable.
It's just not currently in the realm of possibilities for a tattered soul like mine.
I've moved past the point of healing or redemption.
I'm beyond all that now.
Most past movements were never really symmetrical.
I just couldn't measure up.
Unbearable shame and guilt rest on my cumbersome crown that I so deserve.
It's heavy.
This lonesome walk has been rightly awarded to the culprit of an unforgivable crime.
I'm not the man I used to be."

Things I Never Said

—⊱⊰—

"You've become a part of me.
Lovely entanglements beautifully weaved together into the perfect position inside my heart.
You're wonderfully crafted for a lonely soul like me.
Finding another you would be inconceivably illogical and aimless.
My gratitude remains elevated for your act of loving a person of such unproportioned value.
A journey without you would seem like a pointless mission with no objective goal.
The uniqueness of who you are is one of the shining qualities that fuels me.
Your love is embedded in me, and it nicely resonates with who I am."

The Search

—⸺♾⸺—

"I'm in need of direction.
I need a well thought out plan of intricate design to guide me to a destination of value.
Seeking purpose only comes naturally.
Fulfilment awaits an absolute entrance deep within my heart.
These obligations plead for care and attention.
This ache is a reminder for things I desperately long for.
The sound of curiosity comes from directions in a plethora of forms.
I'm confused.
A tragic compilation of artificial emotions leaves me dazed as it paralyzes me in bewilderment.
I need meaning."

Samuel climbed out of the bush the next morning with his body aching. He started to walk down the small, narrow road once more. With the dark clouds in the distance, he knew it wouldn't be long before it started to rain. He walked for about an hour, and all of a sudden, his heart skipped a beat. Samuel heard footsteps behind him. He swiveled around as fast as he could and saw that there was a small boy standing behind him. At first, there was silence as they stood there and stared at each other. The boy asked why Samuel seemed to be so troubled. Samuel responded, "Life hasn't been very fair to me lately. That's all there is to it."

The boy then responded, "We as people have our own personal concept of what we call fair. If you don't have a strong, unmoving foundation for that concept, then how can you be sure you know what fair really is? How can you be sure of anything without having an all-perfect and unchanging reference?"

Samuel pondered the boy's words, and he gradually understood that he really had no standing to call something "fair" based off his own personal beliefs. Samuel turned to address the boy, and when he did, the boy had vanished. Samuel continued to walk in utter dismay.

It started to rain, so Samuel hid his notebook under his shirt. He continued to walk as he looked for shelter.

Samuel walked off the road, trying to find a big tree to sit under while it continued to rain. Instead, he saw a big cloud of smoke in the distance. He followed the smoke and found that it was coming from a house. Samuel knocked on the door in hope to find some aid. A beautiful woman answered the door and asked how she could help him. Samuel told her his story while standing out in the rain. "I'm Sarah," the woman said. "Please, come in and dry yourself off. I'm sure you're exhausted."

The next morning, Samuel woke up in a bed with all-white linen. He felt refreshed and well-rested enough to continue his journey. The night before, he had been able to eat and bathe. He walked down the hallway and into what looked to be the living room. There he saw Sarah sweeping beside a small chair. She looked up and gave him a big smile. Then she invited him to come eat something. It was well into the afternoon, so she decided to heat the stew she had made the night before. "So, let me hear about your journey so far," she said.

Samuel ate while he told Sarah about his journey. He told her about the loss of his wife and all the other tribulations he had suffered along the way. Sarah listened intently as her face showed empathy and remorse for Samuel. She felt compassion for the man who sat before her who seemed so tired and brokenhearted. When they finished breakfast, they prayed and wept.

Sarah cleaned up the kitchen after breakfast, and she washed the dishes in silence as her thoughts raced.

Samuel sat and thought about what was next to come on his journey to Jerusalem. Sarah broke the silence and asked, "Samuel, would you mind if I came with you?"

The question took him by surprise. Then a smile creaked across his face as he responded, "If you think that is what God is calling you to do, then I don't mind at all. As a matter of fact, I would love the company."

Sarah couldn't contain her excitement. She had been wanting to draw closer to Christ and continue to serve Him, but hadn't known what her next step in her walk of faith would be. She ran to her room to pack a bag and fill it with her belongings. Then Sarah ran to the kitchen and filled another bag with food and bottles of water.

"I'm going to need to run to town and say my farewells to a few friends and pick up a couple of things while we're there. We could use them for our journey." Samuel and Sarah left the house and walked for about thirty minutes to a small town. Samuel had had no clue he was this close to town last night. Samuel thought to himself that God always knows what He's doing, and His plans are always greater than anyone else's. Samuel felt like the encounter between him and Sarah was something meant to be. Sarah couldn't stop smiling because she felt like this was an answered prayer. She felt like this was where God wanted her to go and serve, and she very willingly packed up her most-needed belongings and would give the rest away.

As Samuel and Sarah entered the town, Samuel realized that although the town was small, it was busy. Sarah led him to a small shop where she went inside to visit an old friend. Samuel watched as a young man stood behind the counter in what appeared to be an antique shop. He came from behind the counter and embraced Sarah in a big hug.

"This is my brother, Caleb." Sarah turned to Samuel and motioned for him to come over. The two men kindly shook hands with one another and exchanged a pleasant greeting. Sarah explained to Caleb how she was leaving to go to Jerusalem and didn't know when she would be back.

"Well, if this is what God is calling you to do, then who am I to stand in your way? If anything, I should be helping you, little sis." Caleb gave Sarah his horse and cart that included one bag of food and several bottles of water. Samuel and Sarah thanked Caleb as they loaded up the cart behind the shop. Sarah and Caleb gave each other one last big hug before Samuel and Sarah left for Jerusalem. Samuel and Caleb shook hands as they wished each other farewell.

Samuel and Sarah traveled for days. The talked and laughed and continued to get to know each other. It seemed as if they really enjoyed each other's company. Samuel got to know and understand the past of Sarah. He learned that Sarah came from a Christian household, and her dad was a minster. Sarah and her brother grew up learning to treat people as they would want to be treated. They learned to seek God and put Him first. Going through the process of having obedience was always a challenge for the whole family, but being a Christian was never supposed to be easy. Samuel heard Sarah talk about how she had to learn lessons of patience and obedience the hard way, which really resonated with Samuel because he could relate to the hardships of being obedient to God through this whole journey. Patience was also a key then in Samuel's life because he was so anxious to get to Jerusalem. The two of them continued to enjoy each other's company for the rest of the week. They felt comfortable with each other.

Exchanging Pleasantries

"Moments passed with pleasant memories and meaningful exchanges.
Verbal positions of passion seemed to lurk at the edge of each intersection as a sign of what was to come.
Short stories and long eye contact seemed to be part of the equation.
I've never been good at math.
A long-awaited comfort settled into my bosom as I cradled it throughout the continuation of the journey.
Conversations were built like continuous bridges. One after another.
Her smile penetrated my darkness like a single ray of light in a black jail cell.
I can see."

Samuel and Sarah pulled alongside of the road. They had just finished eating and were about to get the horses ready to continue their journey when a young woman approached them from the opposite side of the road. She was riding in a cart that was being pulled by a horse. The woman slowed down and stopped next to Samuel and Sarah. "Are you all okay?" she asked.

"Yes, we're fine. We just stopped here and ate some lunch. We're on our way to Jerusalem," Samuel replied. The woman explained how she was just leaving Jerusalem, and why she felt like it was the best decision for her. She didn't see the point in being there in the first place.

"I was actually living a more comfortable lifestyle while in the land of Persia. Why God would have our people return to a lifestyle that's more unruly is beyond my comprehension. Why would a loving God do something like that? Either God isn't loving, or He isn't God. I've decided to believe that maybe God just isn't real. He's a concept that we have made up in order for us to cope through life. Our reality is what we make it," the woman said.

Sarah's eyes lit up as she prepared to speak. "I believe we see God through all of His creation, and only a fool would deny His existence. Just like a book has an author or a building has a builder, the universe has a Creator, and everything that comes into being has a purpose. He is eternal in all of His ways."

The woman asked, "How do you explain where God came from?"

Sarah replied, "God never came into existence; He has *always* existed. Also, on what moral grounds are you holding the standards to? You seem to be upset because you think God has done an injustice to you, but how can you call these things unjust if there is no God? It might be something you're not happy with, but what makes it objectively wrong? If God doesn't exist, then it's not actually wrong; you just don't like it. The last point I'll make is that if you can control your own reality, then why not make your own life more comfortable wherever you are? I have a feeling you already know all of this, but you just don't like where God has called you at the moment."

Sarah let the silence linger while the woman sat and looked off into the distance. "Well, I had better get going because I have a long journey ahead, but I see your point of view. You both be safe. You're not too far away now." Then the woman rode off down the road with a slight smile.

Sarah had spoken so much like Rachel in this encounter that Samuel had almost lost his breath. He felt like the lady who Sarah spoke to was a bit like an old shell of himself because of her mistrust in God. Samuel believed that in her heart, the lady believed in God; she just didn't trust Him. Samuel felt a wave of relief that he had grown from where he used to be, although he knew there was still much growing in his life to be accomplished.

Samuel and Sarah made haste down the road as it began to get dark. They found a small cave not too far off the road, and they went in the cave and made a fire. Talking and laughing around a warm camp fire never felt so good to the both of them. Both Samuel and Sarah felt a mutual trust for one another and felt that God had brought them together to help each other on the journey to Jerusalem. They ate and continued to get to know each other in the timeless moment that they shared. Sarah fell asleep as Samuel pondered on how much he missed Rachel but also on how much he enjoyed the company of Sarah.

Companionship

"The innate possibility of a substantial partnership with a never-ending contract.
Trust emerges, and feelings blossom from beneath fertile soil mixed with fresh blood.
A blatant disregard for uneasy feelings and unfortunate circumstances.
Lovely laughs and bashful banter tease the old me.
Approved within my inner consultation, I feel free to move forward.
Closing on a causality that has revealed a new road to me.
A lovely prospect in my eye as far as I can see.
Could this be love?"

Samuel and Sarah woke up early in the morning and continued their journey. Days went by as they began gradually running out of food and water. As they traveled down a hill, the horse got very restless and seemed to be agitated by what looked like a snake along the side of the road. The horse started to run down the hill at a very fast pace, and the cart flipped over and sent Samuel and Sarah to the ground, along with their belongings. The horse broke free from the cart and continued down the road. Samuel and Sarah put what was left of the food and water into their carry-on bags and set off to finish the journey on foot.

Samuel and Sarah ran out of food and water by the end of the day. The weather was hot, and the terrain started to get a little rocky. Their mouths were dry, and their stomachs were empty. The two of them decided to stop for the evening and rest. They could get an early start in the morning. So Samuel and Sarah sat not too far off from the road under a tree, their backs to the tree on opposite sides.

In the morning, Samuel and Sarah woke up and started walking on the road again. Dread started to set in for both of them because of their lack of food and water. They didn't know how much longer they had to walk before reaching Jerusalem. About an hour went by with Samuel and Sarah walking in silence. They both prayed to themselves, asking God to provide for their needs.

Then Sarah spotted something in the distance. Her eyes watered as she pointed to the city on the horizon. Just as she was about to tell Samuel, she looked over at him to see him teary-eyed and filled with emotion. "Thank God, we finally made it," he said.

On the outskirts of the city, Samuel could see the construction of the wall. Samuel and Sarah knew that food and water were not far away, and they couldn't wait to see where God would direct their lives after the wall was built. Both Samuel and Sarah wondered what place they both had in each other's lives.

Once they made it to the city, Samuel and Sarah were greeted by many people as they walked toward what looked like the center of everything. A young lady walked over to them and offered them water. They drank merrily and asked where Nehemiah was. The woman said that he was gone for the rest of the week to run an errand. She offered for Samuel and Sarah to stay with her until Nehemiah returned. "My name is Olivia," said the woman.

Samuel and Sarah decided to live with the woman until Nehemiah got back. Several days after arriving in

Jerusalem, Samuel and Sarah were helping Olivia around the house with some chores. "I need to run to the market and get some items for the house. Would either of you like to come?" asked Olivia.

"I wouldn't mind tagging along," said Sarah. Samuel decided to stay and finish cleaning around the house. The ladies left and went to the market.

Samuel was left in deep thought while he cleaned. He thought about how far he had come, and he thought about his purpose for being in Jerusalem. Samuel thought about the things he'd experienced along his journey, such as desolation, loneliness, confusion, hate, peace, hope, clarity, and, possibly, new love. He'd learned lessons of patience, faith, and obedience. Samuel wept as he had mixed feelings of happiness and guilt since he'd started to develop feelings for Sarah. He didn't know if it was right to love someone again in the same way he had loved Rachel. He prayed for wisdom and clarity as he came to the conclusion to not rush into anything with Sarah and just give the relationship lots of time to grow.

As he picked his bag off the floor, his little black notebook fell out. It was filled with some of his old poems he had written over the years. They were filled with memories both good and bad, but there was still a sense of comfort from any poem he wrote because that was how he expressed himself. It was always a relief to write. He sat down in the corner of the room and began to read through the notebook one poem at a time.

Broken Fellowship

The truth is unrecognizable from what it used to be.
Blurred lines and lack of confessions drive me to do something drastically dangerous.
Deceit and disguise lurk around every corner.
I fear for my child.
Lost in a land of lies with no friends and much desolation.
Lackluster planning and loosely-fitted opinions never seemed so unfit.
My vision is mostly unclear to me.
Maybe I haven't built up the courage to appropriately approach the problem.
Maybe this is something I deserve.
She spits venom in the form of lovely poetry to entice me to my own demise.
The fellowship is broken.

Thoughtful Love

I relish in the thoughts of positive equity she brought to the table.
A hand full of multifarious cards that seemed to sway in my favor.
The sweet and savory deck that appeared well thought out for only me.
Never seeming to play it right, but I still love the thought.
Difficulties of finding the right balance to equate into a solid foundation that was needed for something meaningful.
Passed opportunities ride on missed ships as the sails wave a solemn goodbye to me.
I reluctantly wish them a farewell as I savor the thoughts.
Sweet, graceful moments of fun-lit passion briefly touch my fingertips.
Enjoyable for the season, but unattainable for what must be a good reason.

Jerusalem Journey

A lethal hit to the heart chalked up to a learning experience to write on the board for a future reference while still finding comfort in these things.
I'm in love with the thoughts.

Low Value

I'm a worthless specimen examined under a microscope and viewed by close oppositions.
Security remains strapped to their backs as they lug them around as reinforcements to dissect my hidden habits.
I lack the resolve to shape and conform into the brand new edition.
New possibilities and perspectives play a game of tease and wave sardonically whenever I look in the mirror.
Losing my edge never seemed too simplistic.
My value has decreased, and I have very little to offer.
The well has run dry with little hydration and no reinforcements.
A desolate wasteland that I've built for myself as an institution of tight limitations and solid barriers.
Inadvertently becoming a permanent place of dwelling is a lamentable reality.

Numb

I feel something.
Then I don't.
I feel something.
Then I don't.
I guess I'm somewhat numb to it now.
I can't be caressed with the comforting memories of nostalgic stature that once stood in front of me.
I can't be swayed by distracting emotions that keep me stagnant and act as a well-built blockade.
The equity of a life can't be measured or compared to tangible things. The value of a soul we take for granted as we frolic around in blatant ignorance and tote around our reckless hearts.
They don't comprehend the full brunt of the pain that comes with loss or the loneliness that soon follows.
Tonight my heart leaks.
It leaks of toxic acid that melts through the floor and breaks the tile beneath me.
I'll lie down and rest in the commodious pit.
All I really have now are the memories.

Slow Motion

Somewhere down the line I must have missed it.
The opportunity to rise above something more than myself and supersede the last barrier that gave me trouble.
Time is always in motion, and I can never seem to catch a ride.
Blatantly ignored and trampled on.
An invisible doormat covered in footsteps, torn from wear and tear.
Visors shield my peripheral vision while gravity intensifies and slows me down.

Envy

I wish things were different.
The things that bind me to responsibilities that make my skin crawl and leave me linked to a deteriorating chain of events.
Faded illusions illustrate the desires of my subconscious.
I covet that which I cannot have.
A viewing of golden idols I idolize through a plastic telescope with chipped green paint.
My thoughts; I'll label them unfair. For I cannot climb the mountaintop and experience the fresh air and become what I wanted to be.
I envy everything I'm not.

Justification

I feared for him.
Swallowed by the empty depth of pain that constructed his ideals and crushed his hopes.
Pain that formulated his own demise and painted an abstract picture of unknown vanity.
Unlatched emotions and untethered actions probably seemed justified at the time.
Obliteration was followed by pain.
Certainty of equality was faded from his line of vision as he wielded dangerous weapons and used them with reckless abandon.
I feared for our safety.
Pain seeped from his eyes and spoke with his actions.
These steps he took seemed so foreign to me, like sporadic gusts of winds on a sunny afternoon.
There seemed to be an underlying signal beneath his path of destruction.
But he did it all in the name of pain.

All I Have Left

None of this seems real.
A cruel joke imposed on that of the innocent.
Crying uncontrollably for the things I've lost and the good I'll never have.
Deprived from everything except for loneliness.
Happiness appears to be the link to some sort of scattered illusion.
Confused as to what I can touch.
I struggle daily with this constant frustration as I ponder deep in contemplation. Roaming around in a vivid hallucination.
Now all I have left is my imagination.

Lack of Understanding

No one really knows this familiar pain.
It eats with me.
It sleeps with me.
It gives me a familiar company only privy to myself.
I can't blame them for not comprehending my disposition.
How could they?
Back to the familiar aches and pains that nag away at my nerves and scream in my ears. Knowledge of knowing these things exist doesn't change a thing.
I cling desperately for a chance to escape this catastrophe.
I'm still waiting.
I don't resent them for not devising a backup plan for my escape and rescue.
I'll just chalk it up to a lack of understanding.

Out of Options

The escape routes have been sealed, and salvation has been lost.
Motives are unsure, and precision has been abandoned.
Life that I clung to strategically evades my attempts.
Love doesn't feel so close anymore.
Drained from efforts form the attempts to open lines of communication and dreams of abundant happiness.
Devastating epiphanies bring destruction to these emotional walls.
When does it get easier?
The sentences have gone unfinished, and the pages have lost their colors.
The exit doors have been blocked, and the footprints in the sand have disappeared.
Little drops of willingness to follow the highlighted trail, but the map is outdated.

Without Direction

I walk as aimless as any broken compass with tired legs.
I've never been good at directions.
Wandering for this long almost makes the act seem normal.
It seems I have no clue as to where life will take me.
Only questions.
Fear of the unknown always seep through the surface of my mind.
Yet there's always a hint of excitement.
I continue writing pages in my mental book about this long and cumbersome adventure.
Pain seems to be the ongoing theme.

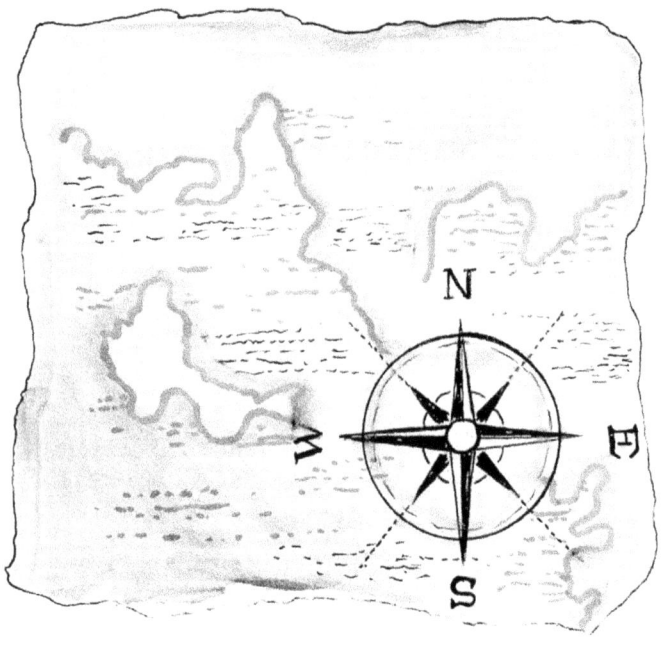

The lonely

I know lonely.
We've been acquainted for quite some time now.
There's been certain times when all we know is each other.
Days go by, and seasons pass, and we're still each other's only company.
We have never been best friends or lovers of any kind; just acquaintances to fill in a gap.
Happiness is always a pleasant interruption between the rhythms of this unorthodox relationship.
Peacefulness is always welcome as a guest in my household, although it never seems to stay for very long.
But I know lonely all too well.

Wasting Away

How much time will I waste?
The amount of time squandered has been eaten away by a vicious cycle that's never satisfied.
The time that has passed has taken away so much from me; I no longer abide by its rules.
I feel sick and incomplete.
Look at how much I've lost.
I can't even capture my own thoughts.
Meaningless is what comes to mind when I think of what might be.
I grow weary of my own smile.
A pointless effort to achieve some sense of normalcy.
I've missed out on so much.

New Day

Things seem to be looking up now.
It's been a long time since I could see clearly.
Standing high above the clouds, I cherish the view.
I can see again.
This comfort I feel is something more stable than it was before.
A brand new breath has invigorated my body and charges me with something unfamiliar.
I can feel again.
I migrate toward things of beauty and purpose.
I'm drawn to people who draw pictures of a happy ever after.
I can see myself in at least one of them.
I'll continue to love and be loved.
And I'll let the bad times in between be a lesson.
I can live again.

A Good Story

The beauty of the beginning starts with a rush of adrenaline at a rapid pace.
Precious moments bleed to the surface instantaneously without a second thought.
The pinnacle of love pushes against my chest in a thorough fashion because it wants recognition of its existence.
I'll oblige.
Uncertainty of how things will end pushes me to fight harder.
It's a beautiful thing.
The possibility of an infinite ending and happy ever after.
Lovely hints and whispers peek from around the corner and show subtle movements of something good to come.
The beauty of the end.

There was a knock at the door that interrupted Samuel from reading. He put his notebook on the floor and walked over to the door. He slowly opened the door, only to find a man with brown hair and a bright smile. He was about a foot taller than Samuel, and he was lean but looked well-fed. The man looked Samuel in the eyes and spoke in a cheerful voice, "Hello, I'm Nehemiah. Welcome to Jerusalem."